# Constipation, Withholding and Your Child

A Family Guide to Soiling and Wetting

*Anthony Cohn*

Jessica Kingsley Publishers
London and Philadelphia

First published in 2007
by Jessica Kingsley Publishers
116 Pentonville Road
London N1 9JB, UK
and
400 Market Street, Suite 400
Philadelphia, PA 19106, USA

*www.jkp.com*

Copyright © Anthony Cohn 2007
Illustrations copyright © Les Eaves 2007

The information about medication in this book is not intended to serve as a prescription or replace the advice of your medical doctor. Please discuss all aspects of medication with your doctor before beginning any treatment programme.

**Library of Congress Cataloging in Publication Data**
Cohn, Anthony (Anthony Simon), 1966-
  Constipation, withholding and your child : a family guide to soiling and wetting / Anthony Cohn.
    p. cm.
  Includes index.
  ISBN 978-1-84310-491-9 (pbk. : alk. paper)
  ISBN-10: 1-84310-491-1 (pbk. : alk. paper)  1. Constipation in children--Popular works. 2.  Fecal incontinence in children--Popular works. I. Title.
  RJ456.C76C64 2007
  618.92'3428--dc22

                              2006032208


**British Library Cataloguing in Publication Data**
A CIP catalogue record for this book is available from the British Library

ISBN 978 1 84310 491 9

Printed and bound in Great Britain by
Athenaeum Press, Gateshead, Tyne and Wear

*For Spolf, Gavriel, Eitan, Elnadav,*
*Opa, Oma o'h and Anne*

# Acknowledgements

I came to poo quite late in my life, learning about it on the job. So I am grateful to all of the families that have borne with me and helped me improve my understanding. The Children's Community Nursing Team has been outstanding in developing our service, and doing most of the work. I am greatly indebted to them, especially the poo nurses, Jenny, Penny, Gail, Debs, Karen, Hilary, Heather, Mubina, Karen, Jannette, Penny and Kamlah, and to my secretaries Michelle and Lyn who have to spend their days immersed in my poo.

My consultant colleagues have allowed me to flourish and enjoy my work in a wonderful atmosphere, and to develop my interests. Thank you all.

Also, to Stephen and all at Jessica Kingsley Publishers for all your work in turning this into a book. To Les Eaves for the wonderful drawings, and to Julie from Norgine for permission to use the charts and pictures.

To my family, my thanks and love.

# Contents

One should always endeavour to have healthy bowels throughout one's life, and one should always be close to [having] a slight diarrhoea. This is a very important general rule in health – whenever faeces is avoided or is passed with difficulty, a bad illness will follow.

*Rabbi Moses Maimonides 1135–1204*

# Introduction

Constipation is very common in children of all ages. It is most common in toddlers. Although figures are quite hard to find, it probably affects up to a third of two-year-olds. It is often a cause of great anxiety, distress and pain for children and their families, but seems to be downplayed by professionals. I see visible relief when families find somebody who is taking their concerns seriously. Constipation devastates the lives of children and their families.

For example, one of my patients is a boy who has a serious heart defect that needs open-heart surgery. He came to our clinic because of his constipation, which responded to treatment very quickly. At his next appointment his mother was delighted and said that treating his constipation had changed their lives beyond their wildest dreams. She mentioned that the commonest topic that was discussed at the parent support group for children with heart problems was in fact constipation. They are dealing with their children's heart problems just fine; it's the constipation that drives them crazy.

The aim of this book is to discuss how constipation starts and to offer ways of treating it, so that affected families have a chance of getting their lives back to normal. I hope that the book is easy to read. Of necessity, some of our discussions will be quite lavatorial, and I am sorry if this upsets you.

These methods have been developed over many years – by learning from hundreds of children and their families who have presented with this problem, and from our team of community paediatric nurses. Most of my ideas and insights come from our families and nurses, and I am ever grateful to them. I am also receptive to new suggestions, and would love to hear of any ideas or tricks that have worked for you.

If you are reading this, the chances are that this is a subject close to your heart. You probably have a child, know a child or were a child with this problem. My aim is to change pooing from being your whole world to being no big deal. I think that we can do it.

For the sake of simplicity, in this book a child is generally referred to as 'he' but should be taken to mean girls as well as boys.

# Mr Poo – A Children's Story About Constipation and Stool Withholding

This is the story of Mr Poo.

Do you know where Mr Poo lives?

Shall I tell you?

He lives in your tummy and your bottom!

And this is quite funny but, do you know where Mr Poo likes to play?

Can you guess?

He likes to play in the toilet.

With his best friend – Little Miss Wee.

Yes, that's right – Mr Poo and Little Miss Wee like playing in the toilet together.

Now sometimes, when Mr Poo is in your tummy, he says 'Excuse me, I would like to come out and play now.'

Is that right?

And do you say 'Of course you can come out and play' or do you say 'Not now Mr Poo'?

And then Mr Poo asks again, and do you say 'It's a pleasure' or do you say 'Not now Mr Poo'?

Well Mr Poo REALLY wants to come out now, so he is getting quite cross.

And do you know how you can tell when Mr Poo is cross?

Well, what do you do when you get cross? Suppose you really, really want to do something, and Mummy or Daddy say 'No'. Do you get a bit upset? I bet you do. It might be a tiny bit, quite a bit or, sometimes, you might be so cross that you even have a tantrum. Well, in that case you are a bit like Mr Poo.

When Mr Poo is cross he starts shouting and screaming and kicking like mad in your tummy. Sometimes you might know this because all that kicking and screaming and shouting can give you a tummy ache. So when you have a tummy ache it might be Mr Poo having a tantrum because you did not let him out to play.

Every time he asks and every time you say 'Not now Mr Poo' he gets angrier and angrier. And sometimes you can't stop him coming out and then he's soooo cross that he even hurts your bottom as well.

Sometimes he will say 'I'm coming out now if you like it or not' and he might come out in your underwear.

If that happens, I bet you tell your mum and dad that you didn't feel it coming or didn't know it was there.

BUT, did you know, Mr Poo is really very nice. If you are nice to him, he will be so friendly to you. If you let him come out and play when he wants to then he will make sure that no poos can ever hurt your tummy or bottom ever again.

And that is a true story.

To help Mr Poo come out there are lots of things that you can do to help.

Have lots of drinks, but not too much milk. Eat as much fruit and vegetables as you can.

Sit on the toilet every day, but make sure that you are comfortable, using a child's seat if this is better.

Make sure that your feet are not dangling. Use a box to support them.

And, because Mr Poo is friendly, he likes you to play at the same time as him. Blowing bubbles can be quite good fun, or you may prefer to blow a windmill. Why not make a noise and blow on a trumpet – making sure to hold it with both hands. You should not blow up a balloon by yourself, but you could try blowing up a latex glove.

I hope you can be nice to Mr Poo because he really is very nice.

# The Life Cycle of the Stool – From Food to Poo

Food enters the stomach, where it is broken down. It then enters the small intestine where digestion begins in earnest. All the nutrients are removed from the bowel into the body as it passes through the small intestine. What is left after this reaches the large intestine and is a sloppy and smelly mush, with a consistency of soft custard. It contains the unused remnants of food and some dead cells from the lining of the bowel.

As this travels through the large intestine, water is absorbed back into the body and the stool becomes firmer. The ideal stool will be sausage-shaped and soft but formed – a bit like fresh dough. In babies the stool would be softer, somewhere between mustard and peanut butter. If you look at the poster 'Choose your poo!' overleaf, you will see that type 4 is the closest to the ideal.

Diarrhoea occurs if there is too much water in the stool. This is usually because it is passing through the bowel too quickly for enough water to be removed. Occasionally, if some nutrients are not absorbed they may have the effect of drawing water into the bowel, which again would cause diarrhoea.

THE BRISTOL STOOL FORM SCALE (for children)

# choose your POO!

| | | looks like: |
|---|---|---|
| type 1 | | **rabbit droppings**<br>Separate hard lumps, like nuts (hard to pass) |
| type 2 | | **bunch of grapes**<br>Sausage-shaped but lumpy |
| type 3 | | **corn on cob**<br>Like a sausage but with cracks on its surface |
| type 4 | | **sausage**<br>Like a sausage or snake, smooth and soft |
| type 5 | | **chicken nuggets**<br>Soft blobs with clear-cut edges (passed easily) |
| type 6 | | **porridge**<br>Fluffy pieces with ragged edges, a mushy stool |
| type 7 | | **gravy**<br>Watery, no solid pieces ENTIRELY LIQUID |

On the other hand, the longer the stool stays in the large intestine, the more water it will lose. If it stays inside too long, it will dry out and become hard and knobbly. Sometimes this can break up and little bits drop off to produce stools that look like raisins or rabbit droppings. Occasionally large rock-like lumps can form. In this case some of the liquid stool

– coming up from behind – may trickle round the outside of the rocks. This is often said to 'leak out' in frequent small amounts, and is known as overflow incontinence or seepage. Usually, children with overflow incontinence think that they are just going to pass wind but get a somewhat unpleasant surprise!

Because overflow can be frequent and very soft a lot of people confuse it with diarrhoea. It *can* be hard to distinguish. 'Reading the poo' is often quite difficult. Overflow is often particularly foul-smelling and usually only comes out in relatively small quantities: large enough to soil, but not dripping down the legs.

A useful reminder is that diarrhoea does not have lumps in. If there is liquid stool with lumps, it is most likely to be a mixture of overflow and held-in stool. This is particularly true if the child is on laxatives, where the amount of overflow can increase to give a 'Dyno-Rod' (clearing out) effect, which can make parents reduce the laxatives too soon, before all the hard lumps have been cleared. The diagram overleaf shows how overflow is created.

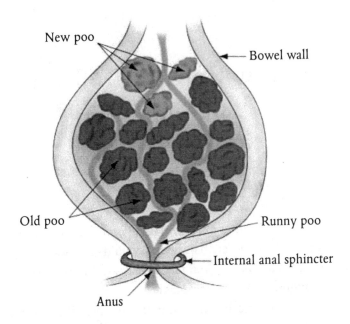

New poo

Bowel wall

Old poo

Runny poo

Internal anal sphincter

Anus

# How Can You Tell If It's Normal or Not?

Normal is a rather unhelpful term, as it usually means 'what I am used to' rather than what I would, or should, expect. If your friend spits in your face every day, this becomes 'normal' though clearly not acceptable.

On average, healthy children will open their bowels daily. But, how often a child goes is less important than *how* he goes and what he does. Passing stool should be painless and easy. In babies the first indication that you may need to change a nappy should be by smell alone.

As the child gets older, 'normal' would mean the regular easy passing of a soft stool with regular being on average, though not necessarily, every day. However, few children remember how often they go to the toilet, and most do not look at their stool, let alone know how to describe it. This makes getting a reliable picture quite difficult. The following questions, though a little graphic, are actually very helpful:

- Are your poos nice or not nice?

- Are your poos scary?

- Do your poos ever hurt you?

- Do you ever try to stop the poos?

- Is it easy to do a poo? Does it drop out or do you need to push it out?

  A normal poo will just drop out.

- If you look at your poo, have you done more than you thought you did?

  If as you pass, it feels as if the Titanic has gone through your bottom, and you look down to see something disappointingly small, then you are probably constipated. On the other hand if you barely feel the poo coming out but then realise that the toilet bowl is overflowing, it sounds like you are all right.

- Is it easy to wipe your bottom?

  Normal stool is soft and will generally – in polite terms – leave something of a residue around the anal margin. This will take some effort to clean. A hard constipated stool will leave little residue and make bottom wiping easier. If a young child wipes their own bottom and there are no left over signs (sometimes called 'skid marks') then again, the chances are that they may be constipated.

## Does it matter?

I do not want to make a mountain out of a molehill. If it doesn't bother your child, don't let it bother you. However, if your child is suffering, then it seems unfair not to address the issue.

# It's Not Constipation –
# It's Stool Withholding

Almost all children who present with constipation don't have constipation as we think of it. Invariably they are stool withholding. If you investigate their bowels, they are working at least as well as anybody else's; it is merely that they hold on to their stool. All their effort and straining is not trying to poo; it is trying *not* to poo. And this, in turn, has lots of knock-on effects.

The whole process seems to start when passing stool becomes painful or scary. If the experience is unpleasant the child will try not to repeat it. The only way of not having to poo is to try and stop it coming out. Unfortunately, the longer this goes on for, the stool collecting inside the bowel becomes larger and harder. As a result, the next time stool comes out it hurts even more. This reinforces the idea that pooing is to be avoided at all costs and very quickly a vicious cycle is established.

'Poo is pain. I want to stop it. The more I stop it the more it hurts. The more it hurts the more I want to stop it' – and so on. The driving force to hold on is an attempt to avoid this excruciating pain and is therefore really very strong.

After a while this becomes a reflex or habit. Every time the child feels stool descend in his bowel, the anal sphincters will contract. That is, his bum holds on. The longer somebody tries to stop himself, the more difficult it becomes.

We can use our bodies to make pooing easier or harder. Toilets are designed, more or less, to make it as easy as possible to open our bowels – squatting is really the ideal position. Children get into lots of different positions when they are struggling with their poos. If they were really trying to get them out, then they would get into a squatting position. The most famous position in older children and adults is the so-called 'banana position' seen daily on buses and trains. This involves standing on tiptoe, legs crossed if possible, chest out, bottom in, buttocks clenched hoping that the train will arrive before the stool. Children will often adopt variations of this.

Even if the child could reason that going to the toilet may not be painful, this habit, built out of a fear of pain, can be very difficult to overcome. By way of example we say, imagine going back to your old school for a reunion and by chance you find yourself standing outside the Headmaster's office. Remembering all the times you stood there frightened as a child will make you tense up, even though you know that nothing is going to happen to you. In stool-withholding children, as the stool heads through the bowel towards the bottom, it will provoke a reflex tightening of sphincters in an attempt to stop the poo coming.

Sometimes this process can cause the lining of the anus to tear. This tear is called an anal fissure. If this does happen, it leaves a wound, which can be easily opened every time a stool goes past it. This can be exquisitely painful and cause bleeding. This will show as fresh blood around the stool or in the toilet pan or on the paper after wiping the bottom. Other complications can include haemorrhoids (piles) or rectal prolapse – where the bowel 'falls out of the bum'.

The overall picture becomes very distressing. These children spend their lives under a cloud of fear. They know that pooing is the most unpleasant thing imaginable. They know that they can't stop it forever, but they can try. The longer they hold it in for, the more difficult holding it in becomes. It requires intense effort and concentration – and stopping it may be painful in itself. Increasingly trying to stop the poo becomes their overriding concern. This makes them so focused that they resent any interference and appear even more irritable and unhappy. If you have a child who is stool withholding, you don't need me to tell you how terrible it really is.

This leads us to some very important points to remember:

- Stool withholding is a protective 'reflex' to prevent pain.

- Stool-withholding children live their lives under a cloud of fear – trying to avoid this unbearable sensation but knowing that they can't do it forever.

- Treatment requires sensitivity and understanding.

- The aim of treatment is not just to get the poo out – but more importantly to change the stool-withholding habit. This can take a long time.

People often assume that it is 'all psychological' as if our bodies and minds are completely separate. The complex thing about dealing with stool withholding is that it involves a combination of both physical and psychological factors, and each of these needs to be addressed.

## When can it start?

Stool withholding can start at any age. There are, however, some common times. These include the first few days of life, weaning, febrile illnesses, toilet training and starting school. The common factor in each case is the stool becoming hard. Either a reduced fluid intake, increased fluid losses – such as with sweating – or a desire not to go, has meant the stool drying out instead of coming out. In each case the stool becomes hard. The hard stool can be painful to pass, which may trigger a desire to withhold. This can quickly develop into a vicious cycle.

Some people find it hard to believe that tiny babies can stool withhold. Yet we know that they can not only experience pain, but also anticipate and try to avoid it. Even premature babies in baby units show this. They allow you to take blood on a few occasions, but quite quickly learn to 'struggle'.

We also know that once babies have felt pain, they become more sensitive to pain in the future. This means that if they are exposed to the same pain twice, it will feel worse the second time around: the complete opposite to the idea that we somehow become 'immune' to pain.

# Are We Missing Something Serious?

Most parents whose children are stool withholding worry about serious underlying disease. Fortunately, finding a physical cause is very rare. A positive diagnosis can usually be made from the history alone – especially if a child is old enough to explain how he feels about going to the toilet. If your child is well apart from this, then there is unlikely to be anything more worrying going on.

The longer somebody has been unwell, the more they tend to worry. In medicine we usually think the other way around. If you have had a condition that does not get much better or worse, the longer you have it, the less likely it is going to be anything serious. Serious stuff gets worse over time.

In most children tests are not necessary. There is no simple test to check for stool withholding. X-rays can show if there is a lot of stool in the bowel, but not how long it has been there for. Having an x-ray of the abdomen involves exposing a child – including the sensitive bits – to radiation, which, although probably safe, is best avoided unless absolutely necessary. Ultrasound scans are no good at looking at the bowel and this makes them of little help in this condition.

People most frequently worry about twists, blockages, hernias and cancer. Any twist or blockage would present suddenly with severe pain, a swollen abdomen and vomiting bile. It would be a surgical emergency. Constipation would not be a major feature.

There are many types of hernias. Umbilical hernias – around the belly button – are harmless and do not cause any symptoms. They tend to get smaller over time. If they are still present after about five years of age, they may be repaired by a simple operation. Inguinal hernias – in the groin – are quite common in children and should be repaired by a simple operation. They are not dangerous in themselves but there is a small chance that they may get trapped. In this case the child would also get quite ill very quickly and have lots of vomiting.

Bowel cancer in children is so rare that not only will most GPs never see a single case, nor will most paediatricians. Paediatric oncologists who see children with cancer all day every day can go through their whole careers without ever seeing a case.

Nevertheless, there are some features that should be taken into account and if present should make us look for other causes. These include:

- weight loss
- recurrent fevers
- mouth ulcers
- feeling generally unwell
- meconium (baby poo) was not passed in the first 24–48 hours of life

- failing to thrive – not growing
- a bit slow and feels cold all the time
- frequent infections – especially chest infections
- blood or mucus that is mixed in with the stool
- liquid stool containing recognisable food.

I would emphasise that finding any of these is very unusual. But their presence means that your child should be seen by a doctor.

# What Are the Signs of Stool Withholding?

Assuming that you go daily, imagine the challenge of trying not to go for a week. On the first day nobody would even notice, as your desire to go would be small. By the second day you may have to work a little harder and may have to catch your breath or stiffen a bit as the desire to defaecate becomes a little stronger. Each holding-on episode will require a bit more effort and this may show as lapses of concentration. People close to you may begin to tell that you were not 'quite right'. By the fourth day you will feel an almost constant desire. You will experience excruciating abdominal pain and an unbearable fullness in your anus. Holding on will begin to consume all of your physical energy and concentration and you will quickly learn what makes it easier or harder, including how to stand and sit. You will find it impossible to concentrate on anything else as the feelings come thick, fast and strong. You will be effectively 'paralysed by poo' – yet the outside observer may have no idea what is going on.

Because the symptoms of stool withholding may be noticed hours or even days before a child opens his bowels it may take some time to appreciate what is really happening.

Clearly, stool withholding is not an easy activity. A spectacle in London in 2003 involved the entertainer David Blaine held in a glass cage, who survived without eating for 42 days. He did, however, open his bowels. He chose the easy option. If he were allowed to eat, but not open his bowels for 42 days, *that* would have been a real challenge.

Stool withholding can present differently depending on the child and their age. It seems that children who start withholding as very tiny babies know of nothing else and so have fewer obvious signs of distress. They tend to just not go to the toilet and will often only be really noticed at a much later age if they start soiling due to overflow.

Babies will usually appear unsettled. They will wriggle around 'stretching their backs' to help keep the poo in. The effort may make them go very stiff and blue or purple in the face. They may grunt, whinge or cry. This will settle as the urge fades or stool is passed. If the holding on is successful, the parents will just see the straining and not the result. The 'pain' can be present for many days and at many times before a stool is passed, and this can be confusing and prolong the time taken to realise exactly what the real problem is. Occasionally the holding-on movements may even look like fits.

Heartburn, due to gastro-oesophageal reflux, is also very common and can present in very similar ways. In fact, the two often occur together. Most doctors are familiar with heartburn and will try and treat it. Unfortunately, stool withholding is much less recognised even by doctors and health visitors. As with a lot of problems, getting the whole picture should lead to the correct diagnosis.

Older children can have the same symptoms, and may also complain of tummy ache. It seems that the signals that most people interpret as a sign to find a toilet are felt as pain by stool-withholding children. Also, these children are more prone to suffer from trapped wind, a condition which, as anybody who has suffered with it will say, is very painful. Some of what is trapped will escape, and frequent passing wind is common.

These children will often show signs of distress. To help stop the poo they may stand up on tiptoe and appear to grasp something – such as a table – very tightly. Often they will go and hide in a corner.

As we said earlier, stool withholding is hard, unpleasant work that gets harder the longer you try to keep the stool in. This often shows in the general behaviour of the child. The longer each cycle goes on the more irritable, angry and upset he will seem. He will be more uncomfortable and less sociable and playful. As soon as he opens his bowels, there is often a dramatic change in character – the rain cloud having lifted. Parents report that they have their 'real child' back.

Although children may not realise that food is the raw material for poo, they are aware that eating makes holding on more difficult. This is because of the 'gastro-colic reflex'. Soon after we eat, as our stomach starts to empty, it sends signals that make the whole bowel squeeze to pass things along. This is why many people find it easiest – or necessary – to go to the toilet after a meal.

Children realise that eating will trigger this reflex and make holding on more difficult. As a result, the longer they hold on, the more effort is required and they will try to avoid things that make their job harder. Eating can be included in this, and the longer their bowels do not open, the less they will want to eat. Once they have been, there will be a massive improvement in appetite.

There are lots of other changes which often only become apparent when children get better. This is because they have had this great weight lifted off their shoulders – or out of their bowels. They often become calmer, happier and more settled. They play more and, because they don't have to waste all their time concentrating on their bowels, they can concentrate on other things. Development and schoolwork often show improvement, which can be dramatic, as stool withholding becomes less of an issue.

In most cases, as soon as we have established effective treatment, you will get a very different, pleasanter, happier and brighter child. One of the most impressive results of treatment involved a young girl with developmental delay. She had a long history of stool withholding. She was unable to speak, but could communicate with a special sign language. At our first meeting she could use about six words, which increased to over 100 within a few months of starting treatment.

I don't want to overstate the case. All the problems in the world are not caused by stool withholding (although I often think that nobody who experiences the pleasures of a healthy bowel habit would ever become a dictatorial tyrant). Nor are all the problems of childhood caused by stool withholding, but it does make a real difference to children and their families.

The impact on families is often great. This ranges from having a child who is so obviously distressed, to the whole family becoming effectively ruled by the problem. It does not take long for everyone to become obsessed with poo. All conversation focuses on whether the child has been and what has been produced. The extended family will often enquire and offer advice, which is usually well meaning, but not always helpful. Although the problem is common, families often feel as if they are alone. Too often, professionals are dismissive, which adds further to a feeling of isolation and helplessness. Relationships can become strained as the problem persists and everyone gets frustrated with everybody else.

Treating the child can make the whole family better. When you don't need to think about poo – or not pooing – all the time, you might actually have some useful time for each other. Parents often ask if counselling or therapy is necessary. My usual reply is to say 'Let's get *this* problem sorted and then see if any other problems remain'.

But the chances are, if you have read this far, you don't need me to convince you that we have to take this seriously.

# It's Not a Wee Problem – Constipation and Urinary Problems

Apart from all the other areas of life that are affected, it is extremely common for children with stool withholding to have some urinary problems too. These children often try to hold on to their wee as well. This can cause a number of problems including an increased risk of cystitis and urinary infections. More commonly, children may overestimate the ability of their bladder to hold urine, with the inevitable result that they wet themselves.

If children are constipated, it seems that the poo being stored in the rectum somehow squashes the bladder. As a result of this all problems with weeing, including wetting the bed (nocturnal enuresis), are made worse if there is constipation as well. They are unlikely to get better until the stool withholding is sorted out.

# This is Not a Book About Toilet Training, but…a Few Tips

I don't know how the miracle of toilet training works. I don't, unfortunately, have any magic tricks. Obviously, a child has to be ready – which is rarely before 27 months. The trainer also needs great patience and understanding.

Culturally, things have changed a lot in the last 30 years or so. In the 'good old days' when we all wore nappies that needed cleaning and washing, and where there was usually a flooring surface that was not going to be ruined by a little urine or faeces – such as the yard, garden or a linoleum floor, the push to get children clean and dry was clearly great. Nowadays, the advent of disposable nappies, wall-to-wall carpeting and fear of letting our children outside has made us wish to delay training until we are sure that it will be rapidly successful.

Many nurseries will not accept children who are not toilet trained, and this often provides the main impetus to start training, but can put unnecessary pressure on children and their families.

It often helps to know that a stool-withholding child is actually toilet trained! This is because toilet training revolves around being 'stool aware': 'Can I appreciate that there is a poo in my bottom and hold on for a few minutes before I go to the potty or toilet and let go of it there?' Stool withholders don't have to learn to hold on for a few minutes; they can often hold on for a few weeks.

This means that toilet training is saying to the child 'Keep the poo in', whereas the message for a stool withholder is 'Let the poo out'. Because once he is comfortable with pooing he will be toilet trained, it is often best to leave toilet training until the stool withholding is improving.

I think that the most important message as far as stool withholding is concerned is 'If you feel it coming let it come'. Similarly, letting the poo go into the toilet or potty can be frightening and can itself trigger stool withholding. If this seems to be happening, it is best to put the child back into nappies and try again later.

Quite a few children seem unhappy at the idea of using a toilet or potty, and will only go in their nappies. This is frustrating for parents, but is guaranteed to resolve itself in time. A number of approaches may be tried.

Not all families are blessed with a respected older brother. I can think of quite a few children whose problems were resolved when an older brother told them that they were being babyish. I am not sure that I would recommend this technique but it certainly has worked. I have also had some children who start using the toilet when their younger brother or sister is being trained, because they don't want 'the baby' to do things that they can't.

More conventional methods would be reading one of the many toilet books, ensuring favourite dolls or teddies sit on their own potty, getting children to sit without expecting results, keeping the nappy on whilst sitting on the toilet and cutting holes in a nappy to be used whilst sitting.

There are natural times for going to the toilet, and these are usually after eating. If you can get your child to sit on the toilet for a few minutes after meals, this is the most likely chance for success. After breakfast is the best time of all, although I know it can be hard to find time in the mornings.

An added enticement is to offer the child the choice between a nappy and a reward. You could explain that nappies are expensive, that it seems a shame to keep wasting money on them when they are not really necessary. Couldn't you think of much nicer ways to spend the money? So if your child asks for a nappy, you can say that if he can do his business in the toilet or potty then he can have the money that you have saved, which he can use to buy a prize. Similarly in the shop, if he wants a toy or video, you can suggest that you have to use that money to buy nappies, but if he can go in the toilet, then you could buy it with next week's nappy allowance.

Children always get excited by presents. A new potty or toilet training seat can be wrapped up and given to the child as a new present, and this may generate enough enthusiasm in him to actually want to use it.

Mr Poo, who featured after the introduction to this book, is an amazing character that children can understand. It can help to explain that Mr Poo has many friends. We have seen that Mr Poo likes to play in the toilet or potty. If he gets squashed into a nappy then he can't really play. And that is not being nice to Mr Poo. If you are not nice to Mr Poo then Mr Poo's friends (Action Man, Barbie etc.) might get upset and might not want to play with you. Similarly if you are nice and let Mr Poo play, they will be so happy.

These last two ideas can be combined so that Mr Poo and his friends might ask Mummy or Daddy to buy you a present because you have been so nice to him.

## Are you sitting comfortably?

Toilets are scary. You can fall in and get drowned or flushed away. This is even before you consider the monsters that live inside them and the crocodiles that can jump up and bite your bum. Hearing the poo splash can be pretty horrible too. Even worse, supposing the toilet is upstairs and you have to go there yourself. And who doesn't find being upstairs by themselves frightening?

We need to make toilets safe and comfortable. We already mentioned that squatting is the ideal position for pooing. Many children will sit on the toilet with both hands on the seat, pushing themselves up a bit. It might look as if they are just supporting themselves but actually they are more likely to be getting into a withholding position.

Children should feel comfortable on the toilet and may need an insert – child seat – till at least four to five years of age. They should sit with their feet supported, ideally with their knees above the level of their waist. It can also help if they blow at the same time. Bubbles, windmills or a plastic trumpet are fun, as is the challenge of trying to blow up a latex glove. The child should use both hands during these activities. The hope is that by using his hands to do something fun, he won't be able to use them to push himself up from the toilet seat – a position that would help him to keep the poo in. Ideally, the entertainment value offers some distraction and the blowing hard helps to bear down and expel the poo.

Some people suggest using balloons for this. However, as balloons are one of the most common things that children choke on – they seem to suck instead of blow – this is best avoided. Children should never be left to blow up balloons unsupervised.

## Wipe and go

If you have passed a normal stool, it is likely to take a good few wipes to get clean. This is often hard for children and so a little bit of faeces in the pants at the end of the day is not unusual – so-called skid marks. Children need to be taught to wipe, and keep on wiping until they are clean. Remarkably, there are some children who do not grasp this. They will wipe themselves once and then finish, regardless of how much poo is on the paper. I have seen a number of children, even teenagers, who are said to be soiling but actually are simply not wiping properly.

# The Holy Grail – Sensible Use of the Toilet

Ideally, we want pooing to be no big deal. This means it won't bother your child or you. There should be no more tummy aches, hard stool, pain or bleeding on passing. Going to the toilet should be easy and comfortable without the whole world knowing what is going on. There will be no straining and no letting off wind left, right and centre.

It is not essential to go every day, as long as the stools are still comfortable. However, when starting to treat I do like to aim for a nice, soft, easy stool every day. We are, after all, trying to change a habit, so we should try and replace it with the best that we can get. We want to establish a new routine, which is more likely to happen if the poos come every day. A daily soft stool also tells us that most significant withholding is being overcome. Often, it is clear that a child will never be a 'once a day' person and this is fine as long as there are no symptoms.

# Milk, Water and Fibre

Most parents will have already tried changing their children's diet to include more roughage. Some children don't like the taste of wholemeal flours and pastas. Mixing these with 'normal' ones can improve the overall taste and the total amount of fibre in the diet. Everyone has suggestions about which foods 'bind you up', but most of these are simply old wives' tales. The chart on page 101 has an excellent list of the fibre content of lots of different foods.

Fluids are very important. In general, children often drink too much milk and too little water. Milk is good for you – but not in excess. Children by one year of age should drink a maximum of 1 pint (560 ml) of milk per day. This includes all milk on cereals in yoghurts, cheese etc.

By contrast, children rarely drink enough water, which is essential to make nice soft stools. It is also good for their kidneys and bladder to keep them flushed through and, as we will discuss later, important for their concentration and learning. In general, children should drink six to eight glasses of fluid a day. This is about 1 litre or 2 pints.

Too much milk is unhelpful for stool-withholding children for three main reasons:

1. By filling themselves with milk children eat less solid food, which means they have less waste and make less poo.

2. Excess calcium can cause constipation.

3. Many of the waste products of milk are passed in the urine. This means that some of the body's spare water is diverted from the bowel to make wee.

If attention to milk, fibre and drinking water does not solve the problem then it is likely that we are going to have to use something else. The next chapter looks at some alternatives.

# Which Method?

It doesn't really matter what you want to use as long as it is safe and easy enough to take. If you want to try prune juice or syrup of figs or something else from the health food shop – enjoy. If you can get enough in, it should have the desired effect of a soft easy daily stool. There is only one rule:

**Never use suppositories or enemas.**

They do often help to get the poo out, but they do this at the expense of making things worse. As we have already explained, the real issue is not about getting the poo to come out, but about removing the fear linked with the poo coming out. These children are exquisitely sensitive about their bottoms, and inserting suppositories or enemas will only add to their concern.

For example, I saw a 15-year-old girl in clinic for stool withholding and resultant soiling. The referral letter stated that her family were very concerned, but that she was not, and this did seem to be the case. During the consultation I noted that she had been seen about ten years beforehand with a similar problem. I discovered that she had been treated with a few enemas. We discussed this and she remembered them as being the most horrible things in her life. I told her that I never use enemas and she breathed a great sigh of relief. She then agreed that she was very worried – especially about her soiling. She responded very nicely to our treatment plan using oral laxatives only.

## Reach for the stars?

Rewarding desired behaviour makes everyone feel good and improves the chances of changing behaviours. So there are good reasons to use rewards in stool withholding. As with everything, it is not always that straightforward, and there are a number of rules to follow:

1.  The child has to be able to do what is expected of him. If the target is too high the child will think he has no chance of reaching it, and so may not even try. In this situation, he needs to be encouraged gradually, without being pressurised to do too much too soon. For example, initially he may get a reward for just sitting on the toilet. Once he can do this comfortably, this may change to getting his reward only for opening his bowels.

2.  The rewards have to be reasonable. If you promise the holiday of a lifetime for one poo, what will you give for the second one? We do not want your child using poo as a currency.

3.  You know when to stop. We will discuss later why things don't always go to plan. Let's just say here that sometimes children can want to keep the attention associated with their problem, and this might serve to stop them getting better. Ideally, as pooing becomes

easier the attention should fade. At the beginning, what usually happens is that every stool is greeted with wild applause and messages are sent to every known relative and friend. This is clearly abnormal, as most of us do not feel the need to publicise our lavatorial prowess – perhaps with the exception of a few men. So, increasingly, as your child goes more freely it should become 'Well done', and then 'Fine, now let's talk about something interesting'.

Often it is very useful to keep a diary of when your child has been and what, if any, medication he has taken. It is best if there is not too much shared interest in this. Parents of younger children will obviously have to keep the diary, but older children may wish to keep it themselves, conferring with their parents every so often. I have drawn up an example of a typical stool diary chart for you at the end of this chapter.

Sometimes, although going to the toilet is not painful, your child may still be holding on. One technique that can be useful is to find an event late in the day that is of importance to your child, and use this as an incentive to help him go to the toilet. It may be unreasonable to do this every day, but would certainly be fair to try it every two or three days.

The basic message is this: 'Over this time you will have had enough chances to go to the toilet at a time convenient for you. If you do not do that, you may have to go at a time that is a bit of a nuisance for you. This could be an activity, favourite television programme or the like. What we say is that if you haven't been to the toilet before this activity starts then you will have to sit on the toilet for five to ten minutes when it does start, which will mean missing some or all of it.'

For example, if your child is going to football club at six o'clock, you may gently remind him from the morning and throughout the day that if he has not been to the toilet by six o'clock then he will have to sit on it then and try to go. This helps explain to the child that it is not worth his while not going.

|  | Mon | Tue | Wed | Thurs | Fri | Sat | Sun |
|---|---|---|---|---|---|---|---|
| How many poos today? |  |  |  |  |  |  |  |
| Where were the poos? e.g. toilet/pants/nappy |  |  |  |  |  |  |  |
| Stool type |  |  |  |  |  |  |  |
| Any soiling? |  |  |  |  |  |  |  |
| Laxative name/dose |  |  |  |  |  |  |  |
| Laxative name/dose |  |  |  |  |  |  |  |
| Laxative name/dose |  |  |  |  |  |  |  |
| Laxative name/dose |  |  |  |  |  |  |  |
| Comments |  |  |  |  |  |  |  |

*A typical stool diary chart*

# Medication for Constipation

If you try all of the above without real success then medication's what you need. There is a tremendous, unjustified fear of laxatives, and I will address this shortly. There is a general understanding that stool withholding will take as long to treat as it has taken to develop. This is usually many months or even years.

The three questions that you are going to ask about laxatives:

1. Are they safe?

2. Will they make his bowels lazy?

3. Will he become dependent on them?

As we will discuss, the answers to these questions, in order, are: Yes, No, No. The laxatives that we will discuss all have good safety profiles and appear to be safe in children. Other than some abdominal pain or diarrhoea, side-effects are extremely uncommon.

## The right dose is the one that works

This is often more than GPs are used to prescribing or pharmacists are used to dispensing. Don't worry. Remember we are going for results here. If we gave a lower dose, and there were still lots of holding on, we might as well not be giving anything at all.

I have said that it takes a long time to treat. Well, here is another little shock. I say that treatment only starts from the time that your child has soft easy stools. So, if he has been on laxatives for a long time with no effect, it is as if he hasn't really started treatment.

Finding the right laxative is a matter of trial and error. Basically, if you give enough of any of them, they will work. What we need to find is the combination that works best for your child. This takes into account the taste of the medicine, how much he needs to take, how many times a day and how cooperative he is. It can take many months of juggling to find the right laxative or combination of laxatives and get the dose right.

Every parent worries about prolonged use of laxatives. A lot of children take laxatives for a short time with good results, but as soon as they stop, things get worse again. This leads to the idea that they have somehow made the bowels lazy, or that people can become dependent upon them.

Imagine that somebody smokes 40 cigarettes a day. If they go to a non-smoking restaurant for a long lunch, they will not smoke for a number of hours. As soon as they leave, the first thing that they will do is to light up. Being forced not to smoke for a few hours will not make them a non-smoker. Similarly, if you hold on to your stools, and somebody gives you a large dose of laxatives, you may not be able to hold on. This does not mean that you have overcome your withholding.

The way to success lies in achieving a soft easy stool regularly in order to change a habit. If your child is opening their bowels daily on laxatives, and has been doing so for many weeks, it can be tempting to stop the medication. If they have not overcome their withholding habit, then they will 'go back to square one'. All the time they have been trying to stop the poo; it's just that the laxatives have made this more difficult. Stop the laxatives and the balance of control will shift in favour of withholding.

This makes it seem as if the laxatives have somehow made children's bowels lazy or that they will only go with laxatives. In reality it is because they were stopped before the habit changed. Over time, the holding on *will* diminish, so that if you see the programme through, then, at the end, you should be able to throw the laxatives away for good.

Put another way, if a child taking a large dose of laxatives is only opening his bowels once a day, he is probably trying quite hard to stop the poos coming. After all, if you gave the same dose to a child who was not withholding he may be stuck on the toilet for days. So, effectively, the withholding child is still trying to stop his poo coming, but the laxatives are making it impossible for him to succeed. Stop the laxatives and we shift the balance so that he may be able to completely stop his poo coming.

The table on pages 52 and 53 lists the most common laxatives. I cannot emphasise enough that they will all work if your child takes enough of them. Clearly the medicine has to be palatable enough to take. If a child dislikes the taste of some medicines, then we can find ones that taste better. If he refuses to take *any* medicine, this is a separate issue, more linked to control and 'who is in charge in this family' rather than the actual medicine.

Parents often disguise the medicines by adding them to food or drink. Some children will often still either recognise the taste and refuse to take it, or, recognise the parental anxiety that can be generated by not taking it – and so decide not to take it. Alternatively, I did treat one child who was on senna-supplemented milk for such a long time that he refused to drink milk without it. He was very much the exception.

Although different laxatives work in different ways, the end result is always the same. Side-effects of wind, cramps, tummy aches and diarrhoea are common to all laxatives. As we have mentioned before, distinguishing diarrhoea from overflow can be quite difficult, and if there is overflow then any laxative is likely to make it worse, until all the big lumps have been passed. Also, the tummy aches and cramps felt by children on laxatives may simply be the signals to go to the toilet, which they feel as pain.

As water is essential for a soft stool, it is vital to make sure that your child has a good fluid intake. Often the more your child drinks the less laxatives he will need, and most laxatives work best if there is a good daily drink intake.

I include a list of commonly used laxatives, and how they work (overleaf). They are all licensed for use in different age groups. I have no interest in promoting any particular laxative. You should always check with a doctor or pharmacist to ensure that the medicine your child is taking is appropriate and safe.

## Stopping medication

Unfortunately, there is no easy way of knowing how long your child will need to be on laxatives for. The answer is that he should be on them for as long as he needs to be, which is similar to the old 'How long is a piece of string?' saying.

## Some common laxatives

| Name | How it works | Advantages | Disadvantages |
|------|-------------|------------|---------------|
| Lactulose | This is a modified sugar. It is in the group of osmotic laxatives. That is, it draws water into the bowel making the stool bigger, softer and more slippery. The stool should then pass along more quickly. | Lactulose has been used for a long time and is known to be very safe. Its sweet taste means that most children have little problem taking it. It is a very 'mild' laxative. | Because it is very sweet, it can cause tooth decay. It is important for children on lactulose to clean their teeth well. This also means it is less suitable for children who find dental hygiene difficult. Because it is mild, high doses may be required. Children who are lactose-intolerant may react to lactulose. |
| Senna | This is a natural plant extract. It is a stimulant laxative, and works by stimulating the muscles in the bowel and thereby makes them work harder and faster. This means that stool is pushed along more quickly. If the stool moves along the bowel more quickly, it will retain more water, and come out softer. | More powerful than lactulose. Usually given only once a day. Can be given as granules, which can be sprinkled on food. | The taste is not always appealing to children. |

| | | |
|---|---|---|
| Sodium docusate | This seems to work as a combination of a stimulant laxative – like senna – and also as a bulking agent. | The same as for senna. |
| Sodium picosulphate | This is also a stimulant, like senna, and may also have some 'osmotic' qualities like lactulose. | Very strong so low doses can be used. Also has a sweet taste. Very useful to achieve a clear out if there has been no stool for five to seven days or more. Powerful.<br><br>Can be 'too strong'. |
| Macrogols such as Movicol Paediatric Plain | Powerful iso-osmotic laxatives. Like lactulose only much more so. They need to be taken with water, so rather than pulling water into the bowel, they keep water within the bowel. | Some of the newer ones for children are tasteless, so children do not even have to know that they are taking medication.<br><br>Recent studies show that none of the drug is absorbed, which makes us feel happy that it is safe.<br><br>Because they need to be taken with quite a lot of water, this can sometimes be a challenge – although juice can be added to make it more palatable. |

If on occasion you forget to give the laxatives and your child takes giant steps backwards, that is a clear signal that stopping medication is not likely to be successful.

In a perfect world, you will have to reduce the laxatives as your child goes more often and his stool becomes softer. You would continue to do this until he was able to go without any laxatives. However, in a perfect world you would not have a stool-withholding child in the first place. In practice, I wait until going to the toilet has been painless and easy for some months. Then I suggest cutting down gradually. If this is successful then we can cut down further. If there is any hint of going backwards then we increase the laxatives and wait to try again in a few months' time.

The reason for this approach is that it can be difficult to know if a child is still holding on or not. By reducing the laxatives we are in effect asking him, or his bottom, the question. If he is not holding on, or holding on less than he was, then his bowels will not be affected by reducing the laxatives. If reducing the laxatives does cause him to go backwards, this is effectively his bottom saying 'Hey, I'm not ready yet.' And if this happens, then the dose of laxative will need to be increased.

It's not always easy and it's not always quick. The secret to success is perseverance. Don't take your foot off the gas. As we have discussed before, we have to understand what we are treating and how we are treating it. We are trying to change a habit, and this is going to take a long time. In general we say it takes as long to treat as it took to get properly treated. Many children will need months or even years of laxatives to overcome their holding on successfully. Remember that it may have been building up for quite a long time before you became aware of it. Also, children that start holding on as babies often take a longer time to treat.

Ideally this should be the end of it. And at this stage you should be able to throw all the medicines away. Please be slightly cautious. Old habits die hard, and if over the next few months there is a trigger that may start withholding again, it is useful to have the laxatives to hand so that this can be 'nipped in the bud'. Happily, as time progresses the chance of relapsing becomes ever smaller.

# Soiling (Encopresis)

Soiling, or encopresis, is not fun, but we can stop it. It is normally divided into two groups:

- retentive encopresis: soiling in the presence of stool withholding.

- non-retentive encopresis: soiling without stool withholding.

In both cases, the children normally claim innocence. 'I didn't feel it coming' or 'I didn't know it was there.' This works as a fantastic defence mechanism as the parents then think that their child has a medical problem and then absolve him of all responsibility. In most cases children don't actually want to soil, but they are aware of what is happening.

Essentially, if you have been to the toilet once then you can feel when you have a poo coming and can do it. If you have done it once then you can do it again, and if you can do it again then you can do it always.

## Playing football by the windows

This is my story about soiling. It also helps children to understand that although they may not soil on purpose it is still not an accident.

Imagine that you are outside playing football by the windows. When Mummy or Daddy see you they might say, 'Please play with your ball at the other end of the garden because I don't want you to smash the window.' Imagine that you didn't listen to them and still carried on playing by the windows. This time they might get a bit more cross when they ask you to go and play somewhere else. Imagine that this happens a lot more times and you still don't listen to them, and then the ball does smash the window.

Is it an accident? Not really. I know that you didn't want to smash the window, but you knew that it might happen. You also knew that if you had listened to your parents that it did not have to happen, and had you just gone to play somewhere else then it would not have happened. So, although it's not on purpose – it's not an accident either.

And how many parents in the above situation would say 'Oh dear, you have had another window accident. It must have been a terrible shock for you. Here's your ball back, you carry on playing, I'll just sweep up the glass and then call the glazier to repair it'? And because not many parents do react like that, not too many windows get broken.

The crunch question here is: what is it like at the other end of the garden? If it is full of thorns, thistles and demons then it is not surprising that you don't want to play there.

## We have to make the end of the garden safe

If a child is soiling because going to the toilet is horrible, then we must first make it easy for them to go. These children are stool withholding. They are aware that the stool is coming but are trying to stop it. Unfortunately they do not always succeed. Sometimes they will pass hard bits of stool, or sometimes a bit of liquid stool (seepage or overflow) might escape, as they believe that they are only passing wind. To cover their shame they will normally claim to be unaware of what is going on.

In many ways these children should be considered as failed stool withholders and are treated as such. They are only soiling because they are losing the battle to stop the poo coming out. The increasing build up of stool in the rectum becomes impossible to hold back and some will escape. Once going to the toilet becomes easier, they will go more often – so the backlog will not develop in the first place and there should be no more soiling. It can seem strange that a child who is soiling gets put on laxatives, but believe me, it does work. At the same time it has to be made clear that soiling is not acceptable.

The other group of children have what is called non-retentive encopresis. A lot of people believe that all these children need to see a psychiatrist, but I believe that many of them will respond to quite simple measures. Essentially, for most of these children, they get the sensation, but are too preoccupied to go to the toilet and thus soil. Passing stool is not unpleasant, so they could go to the toilet but decide not to.

Clearly, soiling is not too unpleasant either. Most of us are continent because the thought of being otherwise is too horrible to even consider. Soiling children often have a degree of indifference to this: 'I'd rather not, but if it happens, well it happens.'

That may not be entirely fair. I think some of these children are stuck in a soiling rut. If you have been pooing your underpants for years and your family think that you have no control over it, it can be terrifying to stick your hand up and admit that it has all been preventable. Wherever possible we try to let the children escape with dignity.

A most difficult question to answer is when parents ask 'Do you think it's laziness?' Well, it's certainly not taking responsibility!

## Not 'on purpose' but not an accident

As we said, those children who soil because they are scared of pooing are treated as stool withholders. What about those who soil otherwise? Here, the story of playing football by the windows is most useful.

In older children I often find it useful to ask their parents to wait outside. I discuss the situation with the child and we agree that the soiling is neither necessary nor acceptable. We strike a deal that if it stops immediately then at the next visit it will be smiles and congratulations all round. But, if it continued then we might have to explore the issues with the parents. It is remarkable how effective this approach can be.

In younger children, or in failed older children, the approach is to identify what happens when a child soils. Quite often parents have decided to 'not take too much notice', and perhaps to reward good behaviour, so the child may get a star or sticker for going on the toilet. Yet the soiling continues.

(We are about to mention an idea that is very controversial in modern childcare manuals. This is that actions have consequences, and bad actions can have bad consequences. Spare me, I am almost about to use the dreaded P word (punishment), but I won't. Let's call it negative reinforcement instead. I only hope that I don't get hung, drawn and quartered for writing children, bad *and* punishment in the same paragraph.)

This type of soiling often happens when a child is preoccupied with something such as playing, watching television or playing computer games. Sometimes they will soil during the activity, or sometimes they will just fail to make it to the toilet on time.

Let's get into the child's head. 'It's my favourite programme on TV – I really want to watch. I know that I have a poo coming but I will try and keep it in. OK, it's getting harder to keep the poo in. I could go to the toilet, but that means missing the TV. I know I'll get a sticker for going but, you know what, I've already got three stickers this week. Watching the TV is more important to me than another sticker. I really don't want to soil. But, if I do it's not the end of the world. I'll pretend to Mum that I didn't feel it coming and she'll be fine and nice with that. I don't think I can stop it any more. Oh no, it's come out in my underpants. I'll just finish watching and then I'll tell Mum, or wait till she smells it.'

Star charts sometimes work in this situation, and are often good to start with. They can prove to everybody that soiling does not have to happen. That is, if the child is clean for a few days or a week, then they *can* be clean. Clearly, if they are getting praised it makes children feel better about themselves and this can serve to solve the problem.

What seems to happen is that they start working really well and then become increasingly less effective. There are many reasons for this. Most often it is because the child is in a win–win situation. If he does not soil then he gets a reward from you, but he might decide that the reward from his favourite TV programme or trying to beat his sister's score on the computer is greater than yet another star.

You have two choices. Either you can keep increasing the rewards or you start playing consequences. This can be quite hard. First, you need to be sure that it is avoidable, and then you need to find the right buttons to press. Here are some general rules.

- Stop using the word 'accident'. These are not accidents: do not excuse them.

- Who should clean up the mess? As this was preventable why should the parents do all the cleaning up?

- Do not become responsible for your child's toileting: if they only go to the toilet when you tell them, then if they soil it's your fault for not making them go sooner. You can advise them of the good sense of going at a particular time, but the final decision has to be theirs.

- Children don't enjoy soiling themselves – we need to work out why they are doing it.

We will explore more of the deeper issues that stop things getting better later on, so I will just mention some simple thoughts here.

The first is that children can be quite clever. For example, many children soil whilst watching television. Once we are sure that the reason for this is because they think watching TV is more important than going to the toilet, I suggest that soiling should cause the child to be involved in cleaning up the mess and the television being switched off. However, some children seem to think that if they are watching a favourite programme, they might soil during that and then alert their parents when something less interesting is on. So they get to watch their favourite programme after all.

To combat this, I ask them what their favourite programme is and what time it is on. I suggest that this is most unfortunate as that is the best time of the day for cleaning soiled clothes. So, any dirty clothes are stored, and the cleaning process takes place at the start of the next episode of their favourite programme.

The technique of sitting on the toilet at a time that is inconvenient for them, if they have not been over the previous day or so, is also helpful. As we said about stool withholding, you may remind them through the day that if they have not been to the toilet by a certain time then they will have to sit on it for five to ten minutes whilst missing a favourite activity.

Striking the right balance can be quite hard. As one mother said, 'It's a bit demoralising if you spend your entire life being negative towards your children.' But I think she may be missing the point a bit. We want to show them that there are many things that they can do that will be good for them, that there are better ways to let us know that they are there and, that if they soil, the biggest loser is themselves.

## Golden time

A good way to emphasise the point that soiling is a bad choice is the idea of golden time. Cleaning up soiled clothes takes a lot of time. If families are spending a lot of time doing this, there is less time for other activities. It also means that the soiling child gets extra attention because he has soiled.

We discuss that each child should be allotted a certain amount of special time each day. If he soils then this time will be taken up with cleaning up the mess. If he is clean then he can have his parents' undivided attention for the equivalent time but doing whatever he wants – chatting, playing or something else.

I know this can be very difficult if there are other children around, but finding time when each can have individual attention is really useful, and you and your children will really appreciate it, even if you can't manage it regularly.

Often, the fact that 'my brothers and sisters get to do fun things with Mum and Dad, whilst I have to clean out my pants', acts as a tremendous incentive to remain clean.

# Wetting (Enuresis)

I think we should pay a brief visit to the world of wetting, partly because urinary problems are common in children with stool withholding/constipation, and, more importantly:

- constipation/stool withholding makes urinary problems worse

- it is almost impossible to sort out a urinary problem unless constipation/stool withholding is sorted out first.

It seems the simple fact that stool in the rectum pushes onto the bladder, and that the nerves that supply the bladder and bowels come from the same place, means that the two are inextricably linked.

## Daytime wetting

Children who withhold stool are also more likely to hold on to their wee. Sometimes they overestimate their ability to hold on, and will start leaking before going to the toilet. They will pass varying amounts of urine, and again claim to be surprised when it becomes noted.

It is much harder to be dry at night than it is during the day. If the wetting is only during the day, it is not going to be due to a medical cause, but is likely to be due to holding on for too long. There are a few other simple causes of daytime wetting, the most common being not finishing or wiping properly. The obvious question to ask is if the pants are wet *before* or *after* going to the toilet.

Poor finishing is obviously fairly easy to address. For holding on too long, the same basic principles apply to this as to non-retentive encopresis, in that both respond well to 'negative reinforcement'. An exception to this is the child for whom weeing is painful, such as girls who are sore 'down below'. These children hold on to avoid the pain of passing urine, and should be treated by making it less painful – similar to retentive encopresis (see the previous chapter).

Some children feel the need to go for a wee very frequently, and need to go in a hurry. They seem to be unable to hold on to urine for very long. This is most likely to be due to having an irritable bladder (detrusor instability). This can have been present from an early age or may start later – especially after an infection or when the child may have been nervous such as when starting school. Essentially, the bladder 'thinks it is bursting' when it is really fairly empty. There are some things that can be done to improve this, such as encouraging children to hold on to their wee or getting them to stop and start whilst weeing. Sometimes medication may be necessary.

Even if this is the case, going to the toilet every few minutes is a nuisance, but not a good excuse for wetting.

# Bedwetting and Medication

Bedwetting, or nocturnal enuresis, is so common that people often don't regard it as a problem. (Clearly, these people either don't wet their beds at night or have a child who wets.) At five years of age, one child in six will wet the bed regularly. This reduces to about one in 15 by the age of ten – that's two children in an average class. Even in adulthood one person in 100 will still be wetting the bed.

Wetting affects children's self-confidence, makes it harder for them to go away for camps and sleepovers, and makes for broken nights and much anguish in the family. The drudgery of frequent laundering or the embarrassment of finding nappies or 'pull-ups' for an older child is often soul-destroying. So let's get a few things straight. Night-time dryness is a skill that we develop with age. We are either ready for it or not, and in much the same way that we can't make children walk before they are ready, it is almost impossible to get them dry before they are ready.

A common theme of this book is that if you can do it once you have shown that there is nothing 'medically' wrong. Clearly with any skill there will be good and bad times and so the switch from dry to wet is rarely without the odd accident.

Children who have been dry for a few months or longer are said to have learnt to be dry.

Some children will start to wet the bed after having been dry for some time, so-called secondary enuresis. Often this may be due to stress, especially if there have been changes at home or at school. Bladder irritability, which we mentioned in the previous chapter, is another common cause of night-time wetting. It may have been present forever or it can start because of worrying or after episodes of cystitis. Other things to consider include whether it is more difficult to get to the toilet at night, or if there has been a relaxation in the rules regarding evening drinks and wees or if your child has become constipated.

If children are wetting in their sleep, they probably have no control over it. If I offered a million pounds to anybody who could wake up in exactly the same position in which they went to sleep, my money would be perfectly safe – you can't control things in your sleep. Most of the time a child who wets the bed has no control over it. Rewards are unlikely to work and punishments are completely inappropriate.

That does not mean that there is nothing we can do to help. Like any new skill, we need to make it as easy as possible to master. You wouldn't teach your child to ride a bike going down an icy hill. For night-time dryness this means removing any obstacles that make it more difficult to be dry.

In order to be dry at night we need to hold all the wee that we make, or if our bladders become very full they need to be able to wake us up so that we can go to the toilet. This means that there are basically three things to consider and these all overlap to some degree:

1. How much wee is being produced?

2. How much wee can the bladder hold?

3. How hard is it to wake up?

# Before bedtime

Ideally, we want to go to bed with a bladder that is completely empty and to make sure that the amount of urine produced at night is not going to be too much. The following are tried and tested ways of doing this:

- Make sure that any constipation has been treated. As we have said before, untreated constipation is just going to make this a whole lot harder.

- Ensure an empty bladder as your child goes to bed. I would ask for two wees before you go to bed: one as you go up, and one just before you go to sleep.

There are a number of ways that we can influence how much wee we produce at night. Our bodies secrete a hormone (anti-diuretic hormone, also known as ADH or vasopressin), which works on the kidneys to decrease urine production. In most children, more of this is produced at night, which reduces the quantity of urine produced. Many children with night-time wetting appear not to produce enough of this hormone, which makes them more likely to wet at night. Giving this hormone as a medicine often helps to stop night-time wetting.

After we drink, our bodies take about two hours before weeing out any extra fluid. Therefore, if we drink just before going to bed any 'extra' in the drink will cause extra urine to be produced at night. So, it is best to:

- avoid drinks for two hours before bedtime; and

- avoid drinks with caffeine – tea, coffee, cola or alcohol, as caffeine works on the kidneys to increase urine output.

All of this is made especially difficult, because children often don't drink at school. They come home and have to do a day's drinking in a few hours. So as they go to bed, they have lots of extra water on board. Therefore, it is desirable to:

- increase drinking during the day.

Children whose bladders don't hold a lot of urine will often have daytime symptoms of having to do lots of small wees urgently. Simple exercises may be of help, as we discussed in the section about daytime wetting. Holding on during the day, and stopping and starting their wee, can help the bladder learn to hold more wee. Sometimes medication that helps the bladder hold more urine might help.

## During the night

The next issue is: how easy is it to wake at night? Some children are such heavy sleepers that they wouldn't wake up if a herd of elephants were to stampede through their bedroom. This can be quite hard to treat. However, it seems that there are a significant number of children who do wake up at night and then go back to sleep again. Sometimes it might be that they wake up because they have a full bladder, but they may not always be fully aware of this. These children will then pull the blankets up, roll over and go back to sleep again. They often wet in this second period of sleep.

This begs the question 'Why doesn't he just get up and go for a wee?' There might be a few answers to this. The first is that he may not fully realise why he has woken up. More commonly he might be afraid of going to the toilet. Often children are simply scared of the dark and you just need to switch the light on.

What is more interesting is that many children are frightened of being the only person awake in the house. They are scared of burglars and ghosts who, as everyone knows, always come when Mummy and Daddy are asleep. Getting up and going to the toilet is quite simply too terrifying to think about. These children might be helped by simple reassurance, by being able to wake their parents before going to the toilet or by positive reinforcement using a star chart or by winning a small prize for a dry night.

A word of caution. I always ask children if they do wake up at night, and if they do, try to find what stops them going to the toilet. I ask them to:

- go when they wake at night, even if they are not bursting.

We then try a reward system, but only for a short time. If they are unable to be dry at night, it is cruel to taunt them with a reward that they can never get. If they wet despite the offer of a reward, it is likely that they really cannot help it.

If we have removed all the obstacles to being dry, and your child is still wetting, then we may need to consider other interventions. If you do need to try something else, this should be in addition to rather than instead of all the things that we have mentioned above.

## Lifting

This is an old idea. Essentially the child is woken up and made to go for a wee during the night. Unfortunately, it doesn't help the child to become dry but it might stop the bed getting wet. If children are lifted at the same time each night, it might train them to go at that time, whether they are awake or not! Normally lifting is so hit and miss and stressful for the parents that it is of little use.

## Ringing dry

Most people have heard of enuresis alarms. They are now quite small and easy to use. They consist of a small 'pad', which is placed inside the pyjamas, and connected to an alarm. The alarms can be made to vibrate and play a number of different tunes. When urine goes onto the pad it triggers the alarm, which should wake the child, and get him to hold on to his wee. It seems that gradually alarms can train him to be dry overnight.

They can work for children as young as five years old, although they are normally only prescribed for those over seven. They often require perseverance and should be given a few months to work. This can be trying, as it is usually the parents that wake more than the child.

Remarkably, alarms may speed up the time to dryness. However, we have only recently realised that some children will wake at night anyway, and it may be that it is on these children that the alarms are having the most effect.

Most enuresis clinics only see children over seven. The alarms can be bought via ERIC – see information at the back of the book.

## Vasopressin (ADH)

As we mentioned above, the hormone ADH reduces the amount of urine that is produced. If simple measures have failed, it can be helpful to give some extra ADH either as a nasal spray or tablets. It is effective in up to 90 per cent of children.

I must emphasise that it does not teach children to be dry. However, if it works, it helps them to have dry nights until they are ready to be dry themselves. I think that this is good enough. After all, if nature intended you to be dry at age 11, then from the age of seven you have the choice of 1461 wet nights or 1461 dry nights, with the help of a medicine. I know which one I would choose.

Because the drug works to keep fluid in the body, the only danger arises if children drink a large amount after taking it. Under normal circumstances, we drink more than we need and the kidneys pass the extra water so that the salts in our bodies do not become too diluted. If this mechanism has been switched off there is a risk of water overload, which can be dangerous. But, as your child should not be drinking for a few hours before bedtime in any case, this should not happen. If your child is very thirsty, a small drink, whilst best avoided, is not going to do any harm.

A lot of doctors limit giving this drug for special events like camps or sleepovers. This seems a bit mean to me. It has been shown to be safe if used for a long time, so why not let the child be dry? I normally give it for three to four months at a time, and then have a break for a week or so to see if the child has become dry by himself. If he still wets in that week then we continue for another three to four months and repeat as often as necessary until he becomes dry. The timing of the week off can be altered to suit the family. If you do want to use it for sleepovers or school trips, please remember that not everybody needs to know all of our medical secrets. Let your child tell his friends that he is on antibiotics that he has to take at night – none of his friends need know any different.

## *Bladder stabilisers*

A number of drugs can help children with bladder instability. These are also usually given without any problem. The most common side-effects of these are blurred vision, constipation and increased thirst, these last two sometimes making the drug a bit of a double-edged sword. Occasionally both types of drugs may be used together.

# If Things Don't Go According to Plan – Theories and Strategies for Improving Results

I know, it all sounds so simple. You have probably tried some or all of the things that I have suggested and maybe the problem is still there. Well, this is the bit that I find *really* interesting. It's a wonderful journey passing through child psychology, behaviour, family dynamics, social pressures and much else besides. All of the ideas have been tried and tested and I hope that you find some of them useful, but I realise that some of these things are very personal.

## Attention

Let's get this straight from the start. I do not think that stool withholding counts as an attention-seeking behaviour. Certainly not at the beginning anyway. But there are many subtle connections to attention, which I have learned in the course of dealing with lots of different children.

I think that the most important concept is the different views that children and parents have about attention. It seems that children think that their parents give them attention when they need it. By contrast, in a parent's mind, there would ideally be endless attention and energy to give to our children – but we all know that there is a limited supply. Let's look at stool withholding from both viewpoints:

*The child:* 'Mummy and Daddy spend a lot of time talking and thinking about my poos. I wish that my poos would get better but I am a bit concerned that if they do, Mummy and Daddy would be less interested in me and would spend their time doing other things.'

*The parents:* 'This poo problem is taking up so much of our time that we don't have any time or energy left for anything else. I tell you, by the end of the day I am so tired and I find that I have spent so much time talking about poo, I think that I might turn into one soon. And the worst part is that I have not had a chance to talk about all those other things that are so much more pleasant.'

### It was all going so well, then...

Stool withholding, as with other activities can be seen not as attention-seeking, but as attention-keeping behaviour. A very common situation is the child that gets a little better, but not completely, or the child that does very well for some months before having an unexpected hiccup or relapse. This gives rise to one of the most fascinating questions that I ever ask: 'If this problem got better do you think that people would talk about you more or less?'

I only really started asking this question a few years ago and I think that it is probably one of the most powerful and useful of all questions. It is remarkable how many children fear that they will be talked about less if they get better. Many children think that if they get better, they will lose out on a significant amount of parental interest. Their life and poo are so closely intertwined, with pooing the major area of interest. They genuinely do want to get rid of the problem, but they worry that this will cause all the interest in them to fade: 'Mum and Dad won't need to worry about me any more' is a very worrying thought.

### Poos or pictures?

One way to address this is to explain that parents are interested in lots of things, but don't always have time for everything. This means that they have to talk about some things, which they think are important, and don't have time to talk about other things, which might be more interesting or fun.

I usually ask children to imagine they had done something amazing, of which they were very proud, such as painting a beautiful picture, and also going to the toilet. I then ask the following questions:

- 'What would you want Mummy to say – "You have done a really nice poo" or "Wow! What a fantastic picture"?'

- 'What do you think Mummy would be more interested in, your poos or your brilliant picture?'

- 'If Mummy only had a few seconds to speak to Daddy what do you think she would want to talk about – your poos or your picture?'

- 'What do you think Daddy would want to hear about?'

- 'Would you prefer Mummy and Daddy to talk about your poos or your pictures?'

- 'Now, wouldn't it be a shame if they spent so much time talking about your poos that they completely forgot all about your picture?'

- 'And, when Mummy and Daddy talk about poos do you think it makes them happy or sad? But if they could talk about your pictures would that make them happy or sad?'

- 'Also, as everybody poos, doing a poo is nothing special, but your pictures can be really special, and they make you much more special than your poos ever can.'

The message that we want to get across is that the attention given to toileting is not only pretty rubbish, but also limits the brilliant attention that could be given if the toileting problem went away. Certainly if the whole thing is occupying a lot of time, then using the idea of 'golden time' (the chapter on Soiling) can be very helpful.

## Money for medicine

Another tactic that sometimes works is based on the same principle. This time we discuss the fact that the laxatives cost a lot of money. (OK so *we* know that they are free on prescription in the UK, but let's keep that between ourselves.) We discuss that the family budget is limited and that it seems a shame that so much is spent on medicines every week:

- 'It is important that you go to the toilet, so Mummy or Daddy think it is necessary to buy the medicine, but isn't it a shame that they have to spend all that money?'

- 'So, when Mummy thinks about her money every week, she says I have to buy all of this medicine, which is going to cost a lot of money. This is really wasted money. Would you rather Mummy spent the money on the medicine or gave you the money instead?'

- 'Well, if you went to the toilet and did not need the medicine, then Mummy could give you the money that she saved.' Often it is most effective to give a small amount of money each day if medicine is not needed.

This ploy is sometimes effective at reducing or stopping the need for medication. There are a few things to be taken into consideration. First, I don't want you to bankrupt yourself, so the reward has to be affordable. Secondly, it is useful to have a 'sell by date' – by this I mean that if the child has not been to the toilet by a certain time, then they will get the medicine instead of the money. The child should be reminded about this during the day. 'The earlier you go the better, because once you have been we can tick off today and know that you will get your money later.'

The other issue with this approach is the 'wised up kid' who realises he can have the best of both worlds. If you give him five pence instead of each spoonful of medicine that he does not need, he might cut down a bit but not completely. This way he gets your money and your attention. If this happens, we can either abandon this or only give him the money if he does not need any medicine at all.

## The devil you know

For most of us, change is scary. We get used to the way things are. Often we don't like the situation that we are in, but still stay there. We console ourselves by saying that the grass isn't any greener on the other side of the fence, but even if it *really* is: we are still too frightened to take the leap. How many people stay in bad jobs or destructive relationships because the fear of losing what little they have is stronger than the possible rewards of escape?

We see this in nature. Animals will define their comfort zones. Once inside them they feel secure. If they venture outside, they start to feel uncertain and uncomfortable. Even if there are better areas for them to graze, they will always want to return to where they feel safe. Not only this, but also consider that there are very few situations that are completely good, without any bad or the other way round, wholly bad without any positive side to them.

Change is all about moving positions, either physically or psychologically. This often requires acknowledging the pros and cons of each situation and accepting that there will be losses as well as gains, expecting that overall there will be more of the former than the latter.

We all know that true change is frightening, even if we want it to happen. A good example is marriage. Most people getting married are presumably enthusiastic about the process, having found somebody that they want to spend the rest of their lives with. Yet getting married is one of the most stressful things that we can do. We have to leave behind our past life and take a leap into the unknown. Although we are excited about our new lives and believe that we are doing the right thing, we still have fond memories of our single days, and are rarely without some regrets about what we are leaving behind.

A child with any longstanding condition will get used to where he is. He will know that members of the family show an interest in this facet of his life, and there may be a number of rituals based around his condition. As regards stool withholding, this may be one of the main topics of conversation between interested adults. Not going to the toilet for a number of days may be another guaranteed trigger for parental concern. Soiling will demand immediate attention, and may be a great tactic for letting the family know that 'I am still here'. The child becomes defined as a poo child. His needs often have to be taken into consideration when planning many activities, from a trip to the park to a suitable holiday. The child knows where he stands, even if he would rather be standing somewhere else.

I do not believe that these are reasons for starting to have toileting problems, but they are often hidden reasons why they may improve but not get completely better. The child does not want to have the problem but is fearful of what things will be like if it clears up. So every so often he may have a 'hiccup' just to check that the old system is still working.

I think the best analogy for this is to think of long-term 'illness' as a prison. Everybody in prison wants to leave. Nobody comes before the parole board and says 'Actually, Sir, I rather like it here, I was wondering if you could increase my sentence a bit.' But leaving prison and getting by on the outside is hard, which is one of the reasons why we have a parole service.

Prison is designed to be horrible. Nevertheless, after a while it becomes what you are used to. You know the people and the rules. You know what reaction there will be to anything that you might do and you understand how the people around you behave. You know what is expected of you. Leaving this almost cloistered world and coming into the outside world, you have to leave all the certainties behind. It can be very tempting when you feel unconfident in your new surroundings to wish to get back to where you are safe.

We all like to feel safe. Children with toileting problems may feel safe when they live with their problem. This needs to be acknowledged. We have to help them burn their bridges to 'Toilet problem island', but should try to use the glow of the flames to show them how much more wonderful it is living in 'No toilet problem land'.

## They don't make them like they used to – the story of the British motor car industry

Another common reason why some children do well for a while and then seem to relapse is what I call the 'British Leyland' effect. This is named after a now-defunct motor car company. It is reputed that in the 1970s this company had a philosophy that it would be happy if 95 per cent of cars coming off its production lines were perfect. In fact it had so many faulty cars that it eventually went out of business. The company accepted a failure rate of 5 per cent and got one nearer 50 per cent. At the same time, the Japanese motor car industry expected, and more or less achieved, perfection.

The British Leyland worker became tolerant of mistakes. If he made a mistake once he could shrug and say 'I have only made one so far today; that will be all right.' A further mistake would be met with 'OK, never mind, I'll do better tomorrow.' Failure didn't really matter, and so became the norm.

Similarly, children may think that the last few days have been good, so, a small lapse doesn't really matter. It is easy for parents to be indulgent at this stage, thinking that the odd slip-up is nothing to worry about. But soon enough these will happen more and more often until we are back where we started. We often discuss that only 100 per cent is good enough, and we are starting NOW.

# Happy Families…and Real Ones

In an ideal world everyone loves everyone else and we all get on really well, The End. In the real world, there are many other factors that need to be taken into account. Which adults play a part in the child's life and which important adults don't? How much time do children have with their parents? How do the adults react to the child and the child's problems and how do they behave with each other? Do they have memories from their own childhood that make it difficult to deal with their child's problems?

One boy had a stool-withholding problem for many years before coming to clinic. The reason for the delay was that his father had had the same problem as a child and remembers his weekly visit from the district nurse to administer an enema. He remembers the dread walking home from school on clear-out day, hoping that if he took his time, the nurse would lose patience and leave. But she was always there waiting for him. As a result he did not want to take his son to the doctor in case *he* had to go through that same hell. Actually, his son was easy to treat on medication.

But I am not really writing about family therapy. Anyway, as I said before, often this *is* the real problem, and making this better causes a massive improvement in everything else. There are just two common areas that I would like to touch on and these are the issues of having too many brothers and sisters around the house and not having enough parents.

## Sibling rivalry

It is often said that the only way to avoid sibling rivalry is to have only one child.

Rivalry is a very understandable reaction among siblings. It must be incredibly hard being an older child, particularly if you have reached a level of consciousness before you have this 'unwelcome' baby entering your life.

When it's only you, life is great. Everything you do or say is interesting and entertaining and reported to anyone that will listen. People watch you all the time; you completely rule the roost. Everybody's schedule is built about you and you alone. When your grandparents come it is you that they want to see.

What a disaster then to have this bawling monster arrive. Everyone starts asking your parents about *it* and seem to have forgotten all about you. You can't do the things you want because little brat needs his sleep/feed/clinic visit. You can't play like you used to in case you wake the little ogre up. All of a sudden they have less time for you and when they do look at you, they are completely exhausted.

They really don't love you any more. Sure, if that little tyrant lets go of them for a few seconds they might talk to you, but you are always second best. It's always 'Can I just feed the baby first' or 'Once I have changed the baby' or 'After the baby is asleep'. You always have to play second fiddle. And then, if you do get a bit of their attention the baby only has to sneeze and they go running to it like a shot. And they expect you to like this thing?

So, what can you do? What about this toileting problem? Yes, great. There are times when they have to pay you immediate attention, like when you are wet or want them to come to the toilet with you. They have to keep an eye on things, and if you don't go for a few days then they won't be able to dote on that horrible sprog, the brother that you really love but wish had not been born.

When your younger child starts getting older and mobile he will need more constant supervision. Often as you sit down with the older child, the younger one will begin to do something that worries you. You will instinctively go to rescue your baby. What does this feel like to the older child? It seems like you will only give them attention when the baby doesn't need it. Like the man at the party who is looking around the room as he talks to you, because if he sees somebody more attractive he doesn't want to waste his time with you. Doesn't feel great, does it?

The younger sibling is often self-aware in attracting the attention of adults around them. An extreme form of this was a teenage girl who had a younger sister with growth problems. The young sister looked 'cute' and elicited considerable sympathy. Whenever anyone walked into the house, even if visiting the older sister they would always ask after the younger girl first and make a big fuss of her. The young girl in turn knew exactly what to do to get everybody in the family jumping off their seats in case she fell and injured herself. The older sister did really love her younger sister. But boy, did she hate her as well. Her frustration was not allowed out because her sister had a 'condition'. The older girl could only be 'cured' when the family dynamic changed and she was allowed to express her feelings.

We have already mentioned golden time and this is very useful. If every child can be given a fixed amount of one-to-one time with a parent on a regular basis, then this time can be used as they see fit, but if there are major toileting issues, it may be taken up with these. This means the child's special time would be 'wasted' as there may not be time for anything else. But, if their toileting was not a problem, they could be guaranteed some quality, uninterrupted time with a parent.

Another fantastic tool as children get a bit older is to take it in turns to be in charge of the day. All the things that become important to your children are very difficult to monitor. Who sat in the favoured car seat, who chose what ice cream we had, who went on the swing first and other such crucial issues. Given the choice, siblings would rather argue than agree as it forces the parents to make a decision. The point of the decision from a child's mind is not whose turn is it, but who does Mummy love the best?

To combat this, create a rota for who is in charge of the day. The person in charge really does make the vital family choices of the day from which cartoon we watch or which pizza topping we have to whether we go to the park or do colouring at home. This helps them understand that there are no favourites, that everyone will get their turn and that there is no point trying to argue about who did what and when; the answer to who makes today's decision is written on the calendar on the wall.

Believe me, introducing this system can cut down, by more than half, those pointless arguments that you have no hope of resolving.

## Divorce

In the last few years there have been quite a lot of studies looking at the effect that divorce has on children. It is fair to say that this is rarely positive. In fact, if you want me to be completely honest, most of them show that children find their parents divorcing stressful and hard. Unfortunately they often seem to be OK on the outside, so we think that they must be all right on the inside as well. It really is important to help children understand and cope with divorce, and give them the time and the space to express their feelings and needs.

Divorce will always bring some disruption and change. Some of the changes will be bigger than others. Very major ones include living and custody arrangements and the fact that children may go for a number of days or weeks without seeing or speaking to one of their parents. The amount of money around usually becomes less and everybody's standard of living will fall. What was normal may now be limited to a treat.

Children often feel that they are somehow to blame for their parents breaking up. They may lose trust in adults: 'Daddy left me because I was bad; I must be extra specially good in case Mummy leaves me too.' Few divorces are genuinely friendly and it can be hard to stop the children hearing negative things spoken about one of their parents by the other parent and their friends. Often there is loss of contact with grandparents, aunts and uncles who may have played a major role in the child's life.

If parents have other relationships this is again very stressful. The crunch comes when one of the weekends that you are meant to have custody is your new partner's special birthday. You want to go away for the weekend to celebrate. Who do you disappoint?

Reconstructed families also need hard work. Trying to be nice to new people who you may not like and who have taken over your life is never easy. Children may play off the adults in the relationship. 'If I poo myself sometimes no man is going to want to take my Mummy from me.'

In children of divorced parents there are a few things that I see very often. One of these is a sort of, excuse the phrase, 'benign neglect'. When you are getting divorced, it is clearly a very emotional time. Your love for your children does not become any less, but the divorce can be so draining that it takes up all your energies and emotions. It is normal to become so wrapped up in what is happening to you that it is difficult to find any emotional energy for anybody else, even your children. You hope that they know that you really love them, but you often overlook actually telling them.

As a result it is easy to give your children less time. They also see your vulnerability and do not want to upset you further. Children interpret this as 'My parent blames me for the split-up, and is looking after me because they have to but doesn't really love me the same way as before. I can also see that they seem quite fragile so I don't want to upset them and I think that I probably have to look after them for a bit. I also hope that they don't get rid of me so I will be exceptionally good so that they don't throw me out.' (Sometimes it will be the opposite: 'I will really test them – to see if they really love me – by being incredibly bad.')

This can often lead to children wanting to protect their parents, who then believe – with considerable relief – that the children have taken the divorce really well. This clearly makes the parents feel a whole lot better. The child may then use medical symptoms as the only acceptable way of getting themselves heard.

I think it is important to let children get upset and angry about their parents divorcing. Most parents actually would prefer to know if their children were really in turmoil. I have pointed this out to many parents who all agree, and realise that they may have had their attention diverted away from their children at a time when the children really needed it. I often use a comment that always brings tears to everybody in the room:

> There is nothing that you can say to your Mum or Dad that will upset them more than knowing that you have something to say but don't feel that you can say it.

If we really want to listen to our children, we have to accept their feelings, and acknowledge that sometimes they feel bad because of us. I know that I have used this in relation to divorce, but it is, or should be, true in all families.

It is well known that children tend to overestimate their responsibility for a situation. They often think that things happen because of them. And this applies to good and bad things. 'So if it was my fault that Mum and Dad split up, I will do my best to get them back together. I know that they don't really speak nicely to each other, but if I have a problem, they will have to talk and then maybe they will get married again.'

It is indeed true that a child's medical needs may be one of the few things that are discussed civilly between arguing parents. Children may also think that a medical need will keep both parents involved and prevent one or both of them from losing touch. More commonly, having a problem is one of the ways that a child can make sure that he is not overlooked.

I think that it is really important to try and support children through divorce. They should be allowed to contact either parent at any time. If they have done something well, they should not have to wait until they see the other parent before telling them.

If custody is shared, keeping a diary can be a nice idea so that each parent can see what has been happening when the children have been staying with the other parent. A great painting or story should also be sent to the other parent so that both can appreciate it. They can then have discussions about what is going on in the child's life.

Sticker albums are good for being an area of shared interest. These are in plentiful supply and involve building a collection of stickers: the child has one album and gets a few stickers every time he changes from one parent's house to the other's. Watching a collection grow ('Let's see the stickers you got from Mum') can form a more positive focus than having only toileting as a common interest.

I'm aware that in writing about very personal issues that are deeply affecting for all involved, this is an area that is emotive and sensitive, but these issues are real ones, and it's far better to discuss them here and realise the problems children experience than to simply ignore the subject.

# Children with Other Issues

I would just like to highlight some of the conditions that I see most often.

## Cerebral palsy (CP)

Stool withholding is seen quite often in children with CP. I think that it probably starts because babies with CP may have difficulty sucking and swallowing. Because of this their fluid intake is poor and their stool becomes hard. Being 'a bit constipated' hardly comes high on the problem list for these children and is easily overlooked. This is a shame. Apart from being easily treatable, the effort of withholding can cause pain and increased muscular spasm.

A further issue is mobility. Children with CP may need special help or equipment to help them on and off the toilet. I don't have the answer as regards wiping. This is one of many activities of daily living for which we have few aids. You don't always want somebody else to do it for you. Wouldn't it be fantastic if somebody could design equipment that might help people with mobility problems get dressed, put shoes and socks on and wipe their own bottoms?

# Attention deficit hyperactivity disorder (ADHD)

Some children with severe ADHD present with soiling. This seems to be because toilet training is a skill that is taught through a mixture of encouragement and disapproval. Children with ADHD find their thoughts moving so quickly that they have difficulty linking actions to consequences. Because of this, success often depends on realising that the toileting problems are a symptom of the ADHD. Improving attention, by whatever means, is usually the essential first step in managing these children. Once this is achieved then they should respond to the general principles that we have discussed in this book.

# Autism and Asperger's syndrome

I don't want to open too many cans of worms here. The subject of autism and bowel disease is one that often raises emotions. As with so much in medicine and life, we often allow ourselves to believe so much more than we can actually prove.

There does appear to be some link between autism and changes in the lining of the bowel, and there are various theories about links between bowel disease and autism. I wish that I could believe that these may lead to a 'cure' for autism, but I am afraid that there is little evidence to support this.

Children with autism do seem to have more bowel symptoms than other children. It's fair to say that they have more of everything. They have more diarrhoea, more constipation and probably more heartburn as well. The presence of any of these can cause pain and misery. Treating them can make a child feel better and be happier, which can, as with all children, have a dramatic effect on their overall well-being, concentration and achievement as well as making them easier to care for.

A major problem with children with autism is that they are more likely to have problems related to food and feeding. Selective eating is quite common, which makes it hard to ensure that they have a good diet. As a result they are more likely to produce hard stools, which may lead to stool withholding. Problems with diet seem to account for a lot of these children's bowel problems.

Treating children with autism relies on the same principles as mentioned for anybody else but they often pose particular extra challenges. For example, getting them to take medication may be hard, and one often has to try with different laxatives in different ways, added to food or drink, sprinkled or baked into favourite foods.

Toilet training follows the same principles but requires great patience. We must set realistic goals at all times. Overcoming stool withholding can cause tremendous improvements, even if the child is not yet toilet trained. If a child has overflow incontinence, reducing the amount of soiling can be a great leap forward.

Children with autism may sometimes take to smearing their faeces on the wall or on other objects, although this is thankfully not too common. There is a suggestion that this may be made worse if pooing is difficult, and the child becomes interested in what is causing him this bother. So if pooing can be made easy, some of that interest will disappear and so will the smearing.

Often, it is the parents or carers that become toilet trained. By recognising the signals that the child needs the toilet, they quickly rush him there, and hope that he goes before he soils himself. If this works, don't complain – it is a great beginning, and can mean that you are doing much less clearing up poo than you were before.

Picking your time can help as well. Getting your child to sit on the toilet for a few minutes after a meal can take advantage of the natural instincts of going to the toilet. If this works, then it provides a stepping-stone to greater success. Certainly any achievement in the toilet should be rewarded. Sometimes this may be with obvious treats, or more specific ones such as playing with water for five minutes afterwards.

Most successful toileting programmes involve the use of simple picture cards, which help to explain the process to children. The National Autistic Society has some excellent examples.

The next problem is getting children to go in different toilets. Introducing them to the toilets at home and school is vital, and it can help to make these as similar as possible, like using the same colour toilet paper or air freshener. Strange toilets can be more of a problem. If your child is going to need to use different toilets, then a toilet companion can be helpful. This can be a toy or book or something else that accompanies the child in the toilet. If you can take this with you, it might help your child feel comfortable on a toilet that he has never tried before.

For those families that really do want to tackle the problem, it can be done but it is slow. It needs cooperation from home and school. Teachers at special schools have devised some of the best toilet training programmes.

If you have a child with autism, you will probably be familiar with the relevant support organisations. In the UK, the main organisation is the National Autistic Society, 393 City Road, London EC1V 1NG. It has a superb website, www.autism.org.uk, which has an excellent section on toilet problems and some invaluable links as well. They also have a helpline 0845 070 4004, which is extremely helpful. ERIC (www.enuresis.org.uk) – 0845 370 8008 – also has excellent links and information regarding children with autism.

## Children with other special needs – and global developmental delay

A lot of what we have mentioned in the section on autism also applies to children with other marked difficulties. With all these conditions, I would emphasise that stool withholding and toilet training are often two separate issues. Even if toilet training is hard, treating the stool withholding will still have a great impact on your child's life.

ERIC (www.enuresis.org.uk) – 0845 370 8008 – has excellent links and information regarding children with special needs.

# Schools

It is impressive that any human being can control a group of 30 or so children, let alone impart knowledge to them. Most of us have enough difficulty trying to do that with one or two. The task of running and organising a school is immense, and perhaps it is understandable that toilets are not always prioritised. However, they are an important part of a child's day, and schools can overlook a number of things. The main reason for this is that they do not always take into account the impact that health matters may have on school success. The two main areas that interest me are drinking and toilets.

Drinking in school is a nuisance. It interrupts lessons, drinks get spilt over the work and it makes children need to go to the toilet more often, which causes further disruption.

Toilets are even more of a problem. Most children hate them and will do their best not to use them – especially for a poo. They are often dirty and smelly, and offer little privacy. Unfortunately, the privacy issue is difficult to resolve, as staff have to be able to ensure the safety of children in the school toilets. Alternatively, teachers complain that children going to the toilet disrupt the lessons and that some children use this as a strategy to annoy the teacher.

Teachers will often think of break time as the time for going to the toilet whereas children call it play time, and don't want to waste this prime period of the school day for silly things like going to the toilet. Some teachers, in an attempt to encourage break-time toilet use, will not let children go to the toilet for some time after the end of break. Incidentally, many schools will not actually have enough toilets for each child to go during break.

Many children start their stool withholding at school. They need to go to the toilet, but find the prospect so unpleasant that they start holding on. The holding on cycle can then quickly set in. The result of all of this is a mess. During the course of the school day children become both dehydrated and desperate to go to the toilet. Even mild dehydration can give them headaches and affect their concentration. This is made worse by having to hold in their stool and urine. It is not surprising to see a schoolroom with lots of children who can neither concentrate nor sit still for the want of a drink and a visit to the toilet. This is the time when they are most likely to soil and is obviously at its worst in the afternoon. In fact, if your child tells you that they are using the school toilets frequently, this is so uncommon that you might wonder if they are really telling the truth.

So, encouraging drinking and going to the toilet are essential not just for children's health but also learning. There is relatively little that families can do to encourage change in schools, but one good idea is to look at the school toilets when your child starts school. If they are not nice, tell the head teacher. If they are fine, enthuse over them with your child and discuss how pleasant they would be to use. It might even help to go with him the first time.

Another point worth considering is after-school activities. As most children do not go to the toilets at school, lots of children are holding on and head for the toilet as soon as they get home – they know that they can just about do it. If they are taken straight to an after-school visit, this may exceed their holding-on powers. Many a trip to the shoe shop is marred by soiling, because the child thought he would be going straight home. So, if you are going out after school, remember to ask if anyone might need the toilet.

Prevention is always better than cure. The best time to go to the toilet is in the morning. In fact after breakfast is the 'natural time' for a poo. Our bowels have had all night to digest our suppers and eating breakfast triggers the gastro-colic reflex. Hey presto, it's happy hour for Mr Poo. Let him out then, and he won't bother you during the day, so the question of having to go to the toilet at school won't even arise. Training children to go to the toilet in the morning is really valuable. Having the time in the morning to do this can be a rare luxury.

## Conclusion

I hope that this book has been helpful. If you find yourself struggling with your child, please remember that you are not alone: up to 30 per cent of toddlers have this problem and there are plenty of networks and sources of advice out there – some of which are listed in the 'Contacts and Further Information' chapter. Try to keep in mind that if you can stick with the programme it will eventually get better. And when it does get better everybody's life will be transformed.

If you have any comments or ideas I would love to hear them. I have learned a great deal through my work with families, but am always interested to hear new viewpoints or experiences.

# Appendix

# A High Fibre Diet

A high fibre and fluid diet is a healthy diet that is suitable for all the family. You should encourage a regular meal pattern and increase the whole family's fibre and fluid intake at every meal. By doing this you will increase the water content of stools, making them softer and easier to pass.

## How to calculate how much fibre your child should be eating

For children older than two years, calculate (Age) + 5 grams per day, e.g. if your child is seven years old, the calculation would be 7 + 5 = 12 grams per day.

| Food | Portion size | Fibre content (grams) |
|------|-------------|----------------------|
| **Bread** | | |
| Wholemeal | 1 small slice | 1.5 |
| Brown | 1 small slice | 0.9 |
| Hovis | 1 small slice | 0.8 |
| High fibre white | 1 small slice | 0.8 |
| Wholemeal pitta bread | 1 mini | 1.8 |

*Continued on next page*

| Food | Portion size | Fibre content (grams) |
|------|--------------|------------------------|
| **Breakfast cereals** | | |
| All-Bran | Average small bowl | 7.2 |
| Bran Buds | Average small bowl | 6.6 |
| Mini Shredded Wheat | Average small bowl | 3.4 |
| Bran Flakes | Average small bowl | 2.6 |
| Sultana Bran | Average small bowl | 2.0 |
| Fruit 'n' Fibre | Average small bowl | 1.4 |
| Country Store | Average small bowl | 1.2 |
| Raisin Splitz | Average small bowl | 2.3 |
| Corn Flakes | Average small bowl | 0.2 |
| Muesli | Average small bowl | 2 |
| Weetabix | 1 biscuit | 1.9 |
| **Biscuits and pastry** | | |
| Cracker (wholemeal) | 1 | 0.4 |
| Digestive (plain) | 1 | 0.3 |
| Gingernuts | 1 | 0.2 |
| Oatcakes | 1 | 0.7 |

| Food | Portion size | Fibre content (grams) |
|---|---|---|
| Shortbread | 1 | 0.2 |
| Oat based biscuit | 1 | 0.5 |
| Wholemeal scone | Average size (1) | 2.6 |
| Wholemeal fruit cake | Average slice | 1.7 |
| Cereal bar | 1 | 1.0 |
| **Fruit (raw)** | | |
| Apple | 1 small | 1.3 |
| Avocado pear | ½ | 2.6 |
| Banana | 1 medium | 1.1 |
| Blackberries | 10 | 1.55 |
| Dates (dried) | 5 | 3.0 |
| Fruit cocktail (canned in juice) | Small bowl | 1.2 |
| Grapefruit | ½ | 1.0 |
| Grapes | 10 | 0.6 |
| Kiwi fruit | 1 medium | 1.1 |
| Mango | 1 slice | 1.0 |
| Melon (cantaloupe) | 1 slice | 1.5 |
| Orange | 1 small | 2.0 |
| Peach | 1 small | 1.1 |
| Pear | 1 medium | 3.3 |
| Pineapple | 1 large slice | 1.0 |
| Plum | 1 small | 0.5 |

*Continued on next page*

| Food | Portion size | Fibre content (grams) |
|---|---|---|
| Prunes (dried) | 5 | 2.3 |
| Raisins | 1 tablespoon | 0.6 |
| Raspberries | 10 | 1.0 |
| Tangerine | 1 small | 0.6 |
| Strawberries | 5 | 0.7 |
| Sultanas | 24 | 0.5 |
| **Nuts\*** | | |
| Almonds | 6 whole | 1.0 |
| Brazils | 3 whole | 0.6 |
| Peanuts | 10 whole | 0.8 |
| Peanut butter | Thickly spread on 1 slice bread | 1.4 |
| **Rice and pasta** | | |
| Brown boiled rice | 2 heaped tablespoons | 0.6 |
| Wholemeal spaghetti | 3 tablespoons | 3.1 |
| **Vegetables** | | |
| Carrots | 2 tablespoons | 2 |
| Beetroot | 4 slices | 0.8 |
| Turnip | 1 tablespoon | 0.8 |
| Potatoes – baked with skin | Small | 2.7 |
| Potatoes – new | 2 average | 1.2 |

\*Nuts should not be given to children under five years due to the risk of choking

| Food | Portion size | Fibre content (grams) |
|---|---|---|
| Oven chips | Small portion | 1.2 |
| Spinach | 2 tablespoons | 1.7 |
| Broccoli tops (raw) | 2 spears | 2.4 |
| Cabbage | 2 tablespoons | 1.1 |
| Cauliflower | 3 florets | 0.5 |
| Celery (raw) | 1 stick | 0.3 |
| Leeks | Stem, white portion only | 1.1 |
| Peas | 2 tablespoons | 3.0 |
| Broad beans | 2 tablespoons | 7.8 |
| Butter beans | 2 tablespoons | 3.7 |
| Red kidney beans | 2 tablespoons | 4.3 |
| Chickpeas | 2 tablespoons | 2.9 |
| Baked beans | 2 tablespoons | 3.0 |
| Lentils – split (boiled) | 2 tablespoons | 1.5 |
| Corn-on-the-cob | 1 whole | 2.7 |
| Sweetcorn – can | 2 tablespoons | 0.9 |
| Tomatoes – raw | 1 small | 0.7 |
| Green pepper | 2 sliced rings | 0.3 |

# Contacts and Further Information

## United Kingdom

I would highly recommend getting in touch with:

**ERIC – Education and Resources for Improving Childhood Continence (www.enuresis.org.uk)**
34 Old School House, Britannia Road
Kingswood
Bristol BS15 8DB
Tel: 0845 370 8008

It has an excellent website and a parent support line.

**The National Autistic Society (www.autism.org.uk)**
393 City Road
London EC1V 1NG
Tel: 020 7833 2299

Great links to toileting.

**Disabled Living (www.disabledliving.co.uk)**
Redbank House, 4 St Chad's Street
Cheetham
Manchester M8 8QA
Tel: 0870 777 4714
E-mail: info@disabledliving.co.uk

Lots of information and resources.

**www.childhoodconstipation.com**

Produced by one of the laxative companies, but is nevertheless a good site, including nice pictures and a food fibre chart.

## Australia
**Children, Youth and Women's Health Service (www.cyh.com)**

Has information easily understood by children.

**www.healthinsite.gov.au**

Also good – put in 'childhood constipation' for the search.

## USA
**www.med.umich.edu**
University of Michigan Health System
1500 E. Medical Center Drive
Ann Arbor
MI 48109
Tel: 001 734 936 4000

Contains useful links and some further reading.

## Books

There are lots of good books on the digestive system and toilet training. A perennial favourite for anybody who is unhappy with poos is *Everybody Poos* (2002) by Taro Gomi (London: Frances Lincoln Children's Books).

# Index